EXPLORING
SPACE

ANNE ROONEY

D1387117

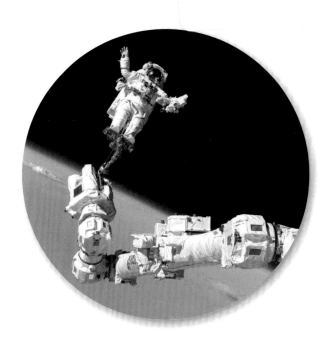

Badger Publishing Limited
Oldmedow Road,
Hardwick Industrial Estate,
King's Lynn PE30 4JJ
Telephone: 01438 791037

www.badgerlearning.co.uk

4 6 8 10 9 7 5 3

Exploring Space ISBN 978-1-78464-042-2

Text © Anne Rooney 2014
Complete work © Badger Publishing Limited 2014

All rights reserved. No part of this publication may be reproduced, stored in any form
or by any means mechanical, electronic, recording or otherwise without the prior
permission of the publisher.

The right of Anne Rooney to be identified as author of this work has been asserted
by her in accordance with the Copyright, Designs and Patents Act 1988.

Publisher: Susan Ross
Senior Editor: Danny Pearson
Publishing Assistant: Claire Morgan
Designer: Fiona Grant
Series Consultant: Dee Reid

Photos: Cover image: Sipa Press/REX
Page 5: © Aflo Co., Ltd./Alamy
Page 6: REX
Page 7: Universal History Archive/REX
Page 8: NASA images
Page 9: KeystoneUSA-ZUMA/REX
Page 10: Sovfoto/Universal Images Gro/REX
Page 11: NASA images
Page 12: Sovfoto/Universal Images Gro/REX
Page 13: NASA images
Page 14: NASA images
Page 15: Sovfoto/Universal Images Gro/REX
Page 16: NASA images
Page 17: NASA images
Page 18: Imaginechina/REX
Page 20: NASA images
Page 21: NASA images
Page 22: NASA images
Page 23: NASA images
Page 24: Image Broker/REX
Page 25: NASA images
Page 26: NASA images
Page 27: © epa european pressphoto agency b.v/Alamy
Page 28: NASA/JPL
Page 29: © J Marshall - Tribaleye Images/Alamy
Page 30: © Stocktrek Images, Inc./Alamy

Attempts to contact all copyright holders have been made.
If any omitted would care to contact Badger Learning, we will be happy to make appropriate arrangements.

EXPLORING SPACE

Contents

Badger
LEARNING

Vocabulary

astronauts	spacecraft
atmosphere	Sputnik
exoplanets	telescope
experiments	unmanned

1. STARING INTO SPACE

Long ago, people explained the stars by telling stories of gods and heroes.

The Ancient Greeks saw the figure of Orion the hunter in these stars.

Then, 500 years ago, the first telescopes showed the truth. The planets are other worlds. The stars are other suns, trillions of kilometres away.

2. BLAST OFF

As people discovered more about the moon, stars and planets, they began to dream of travelling into space.

First rockets
The very first rocket was made by the American Robert H. Goddard in 1926.

WOW! facts

His first tiny rocket flew for only 2.5 seconds, and only went 12.5 metres off the ground!

In 1934, the German scientist Wernher von Braun was more successful.

He launched two rockets and one of them reached a height of 3.5 kilometres.

He had always said that his dream was to visit the moon. People call him the father of rocket science.

Germany was getting ready for the Second World War.

The German government made von Braun turn his rockets into weapons.

His A-4 rocket became famous as the V-2 missile, used to bomb Britain.

After the war, von Braun moved to the USA. He worked first on rocket planes and then on the new space programme, which became The North American Space Agency (NASA).

How a rocket works
Fuel is mixed with air or
oxygen in the rocket.
It burns at a very high
temperature.

The gases produced expand
and are forced out of the
nozzle at the back of the
rocket and the rocket
zooms up.

3. OUT OF THIS WORLD

Von Braun's V-2 rocket was the first to go high enough to reach space.

But the first rocket to carry something else into space was launched in 1957.

The USSR used an R-7 ICBM rocket to carry the first man-made satellite into space. It was called Sputnik.

Sputnik was a metal sphere 58 centimetres across with four radio aerials.

It went around the Earth at 29,000 kilometres per hour. Each orbit took just 96 minutes.

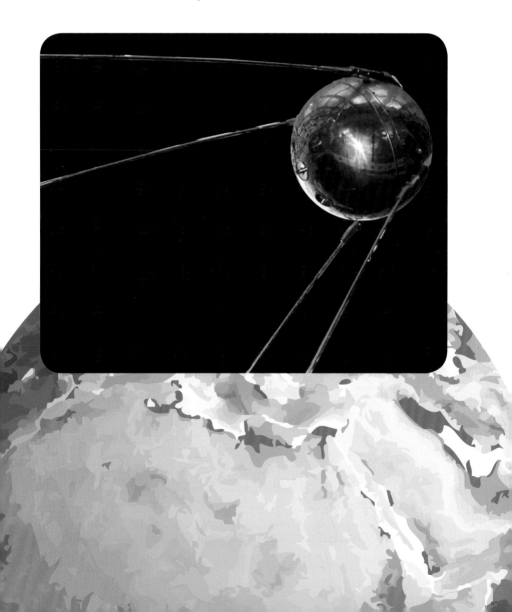

Spaceman

After sending a satellite into space, the next challenge was to send a human into space.

The USSR did that on 12th April 1961.

Yuri Gagarin was
the first man
in space.

When Gagarin was asked what he saw in space he said:

"I saw for the first time the Earth's shape. I could easily see the shores of continents, islands, great rivers... The horizon is dark blue, smoothly turning to black."

WOW! facts

His flight in Vostok 1 took one hour 48 minutes and made one orbit of earth.

Space race

After Sputnik and Vostok 1, the USSR and USA raced to explore space and put a human on the moon.

They both sent probes, which are spacecraft with no crew, to the planet Venus. Venus is the second planet from the sun.

In 1962 the American spacecraft Mariner 2 flew close to Venus and took photos.

In 1970 the USSR spacecraft Venera 7 landed on Venus.

Venus has a very hot, acidic atmosphere with fierce storms.

It was not easy for spacecraft to land.

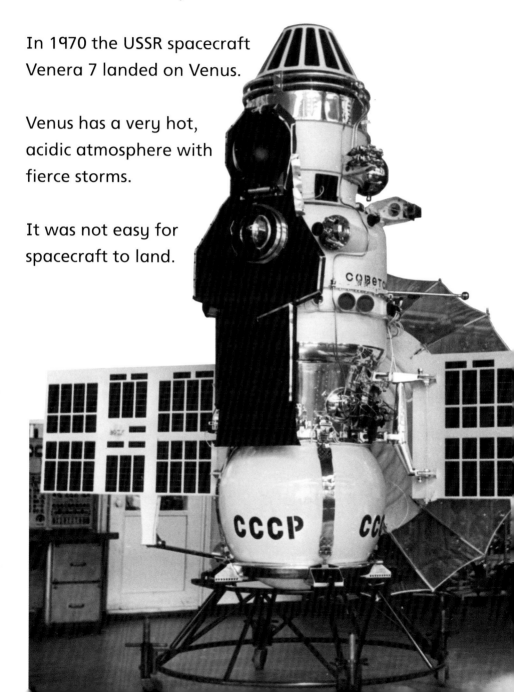

4. MISSIONS TO THE MOON

The USA won the space race to land a human on the moon!

On 20th July 1969 Apollo 11 was launched by a Saturn V rocket.

Neil Armstrong and Buzz Aldrin became the first people ever to step on ground outside Earth.

When Neil Armstrong took the first step onto the moon he said:

"That's one small step for a man – one giant leap for mankind."

The North American Space Agency (NASA) made five more manned moon landings.

WOW! facts

The last moon landing was in 1972.

What did the astronauts do on the moon?

1. They took photos.
2. They did experiments.
3. They collected moon rock and dust.

Since 1972, unmanned probes have been to the moon to do more research. There were no landings from 1976 to 2013.

In 2013 the Chinese rover Jade Rabbit landed on the moon.

Important moon missions

Date	Country	Craft	Mission
4/1/59	USSR	Luna 1	Flyby
14/9/59	USSR	Luna 2	Crashed onto the moon
3/2/66	USSR	Luna 9	First 'soft' landing
20/7/69	USA	Apollo 11	First men on the moon
14/12/13	China	Chang'e 3	Jade Rabbit rover starts a year-long mission

5. LIVING IN SPACE

Spacecraft don't always go to another planet or the moon. Some go into space and stay there.

Space stations orbit the Earth. At the moment, there is one working space station.

It is called the International Space Station or the ISS. Astronauts travel to the ISS by space shuttle.

They live on the space station for weeks or months carrying out experiments.

Sometimes astronauts need to work on the outside of the space station. They do this during a spacewalk.

Seeing stars

The Hubble Space Telescope is a very powerful telescope.

It is in orbit around the Earth. It takes clear images of objects very far away in space. It sends photos back to Earth by computer link.

If something goes wrong with the Hubble Telescope it is mended by astronauts in space.

Another telescope, called Kepler, also orbits Earth.

It looks for planets going around distant stars. These are called exoplanets.

Scientists want to know more about exoplanets. There might even be alien life on some of them.

6. NEXT STOP MARS

Mars is the planet most like Earth in our solar system.

It has a rocky surface and it is almost the same size as Earth. Some scientists hope we might be able to build a base on Mars.

No astronauts have visited Mars yet, but we have sent rovers.

Rovers are robotic vehicles controlled by computers on Earth.

What do the rovers do on Mars?

1. The rovers collect rock and dust.
2. They take photographs.
3. They test the planet to look for gases that might be signs of life.

Could humans ever travel to Mars? How difficult would it be?

- It would take around nine months to get there.

- Then the astronauts would have to wait for Mars and Earth to be in the right places in orbit before they could come back.

- The whole trip would take about two years.

- The spaceship would have to carry all the food and water that would be needed for two years.

- We don't know how humans could manage on Mars. There could be health risks.

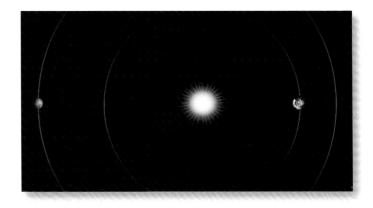

But a trip to Mars might happen one day. NASA hopes to send a crew to Mars in the 2020s.

Would you like to be on board?

7. INTO THE UNKNOWN

In 1979, The Voyager 1 spacecraft was launched from Earth.

It is now 19 billion kilometres from Earth. That is far beyond any of the planets in our solar system!

This is a picture of Earth taken by Voyager 1 from over 6.4 billion kilometres away. Just imagine what it looks like now!

What is on board Voyager 1?

Voyager carries a 'Golden Record', which has these sounds and photos from Earth:

- a baby crying
- whales singing
- waves crashing on a shore
- all kinds of music from classical to modern

There are also greetings in 66 Earth languages to any aliens that find Voyager.

How would you describe our world to an alien?

Looking for life

There are a lot of exoplanets out in space. Scientists have found thousands already. There might be alien life on some of them. If there is water on a planet and it is not too close to or too far away from its sun, then something might live on it. Maybe one day we will find out.

Questions

Who made the very first rocket? *(page 6)*

What was the first man-made satellite in space called? *(page 10)*

What was the name of the spacecraft that landed on Venus? *(page 15)*

How many manned moon landings has NASA made in total? *(page 17)*

What does the telescope called Kepler look for? *(page 23)*

How far is Voyager 1 from Earth? *(page 28)*

INDEX